I0877559

Wildlife Cable
AFGHANS

With these classic afghans featuring silhouettes of a bear, moose, wolf, and deer, it's easy to imagine yourself on vacation deep in the woods. The interchangeable side panels and corner squares offer lots of possible design combinations.

The Bear Chart, Square One, and Panel One were used to create the afghan on this page.

LEISURE ARTS, INC. • Maumelle, Arkansas

Wildlife Afghan

Afghan is constructed of one Center Panel, 2 short and 2 long Side Panels, and 4 Corner Squares. Choose and combine your favorite patterns to make your one-of-a-kind Afghan!

INTERMEDIATE

Finished Size: 35½" x 44¾" (90 cm x 113.5 cm)

SHOPPING LIST

Yarn (Medium Weight) 4 MEDIUM

[5 ounces, 251 yards
(142 grams, 230 meters) per skein]:

- ☐ Main Color (MC) - 6 skeins

[6 ounces, 315 yards
(170 grams, 288 meters) per skein]:

- ☐ Contrasting Color (CC) - 2 skeins

Crochet Hooks

- ☐ Size H (5 mm) **and**
- ☐ Size I (5.5 mm)
  or sizes needed for gauge

Additional Supplies

- ☐ Yarn needle

GAUGE INFORMATION

With smaller size hook,
16 hdc and 13 rows = 4" (10 cm)
With larger size hook,
15 hdc and 11 rows = 4" (10 cm)

Gauge Swatch #1: 4" (10 cm) square
With smaller size hook and CC, ch 17.
Row 1: Hdc in third ch from hook **(2 skipped chs count as first hdc)** and in each ch across: 16 hdc.
Rows 2-13: Ch 2 **(counts as first hdc)**, turn; hdc in next hdc and in each hdc across.
Finish off.

Gauge Swatch #2: 4" (10 cm) square
With larger size hook and MC, ch 16.
Row 1: Hdc in third ch from hook **(2 skipped chs count as first hdc)** and in each ch across: 15 hdc.
Rows 2-11: Ch 2 **(counts as first hdc)**, turn; hdc in next hdc and in each hdc across.
Finish off.

The Deer Chart, Square Three, and Panel Four were used to create the afghan on page 2.

STITCH GUIDE

TREBLE CROCHET ***(abbreviated tr)***

YO twice, insert hook in st indicated, YO and pull up a loop (4 loops on hook), (YO and draw through 2 loops on hook) 3 times.

CROSS ST (uses next 2 sts)

Skip next st, hdc in next st, working **around** hdc just made, hdc in skipped st.

SINGLE CROCHET 2 TOGETHER ***(abbreviated sc2tog)***

Pull up a loop in each of next 2 sts, YO and draw through all 3 loops on hook (**counts as one sc**).

BACK POST DOUBLE CROCHET ***(abbreviated BPdc)***

YO, insert hook from **back** to **front** around post of st indicated ***(Fig. 3, page 31)***, YO and pull up a loop (3 loops on hook), (YO and draw through 2 loops on hook) twice.

FRONT POST DOUBLE CROCHET ***(abbreviated FPdc)***

YO, insert hook from **front** to **back** around post of st indicated ***(Fig. 3, page 31)***, YO and pull up a loop (3 loops on hook), (YO and draw through 2 loops on hook) twice. Skip st **behind** FPdc.

FRONT POST TREBLE CROCHET***(abbreviated FPtr)***

YO twice, insert hook from **front** to **back** around post of FPst indicated 2 rows **below** ***(Fig. 3, page 31)***, YO and pull up a loop (4 loops on hook), (YO and draw through 2 loops on hook) 3 times. Skip st **behind** FPtr unless otherwise indicated.

FRONT POST CLUSTER ***(abbreviated FP Cluster)***

(worked around post of one st)

★ YO, insert hook from **front** to **back** around post of st indicated ***(Fig. 3, page 31)***, YO and pull up a loop, YO and draw through 2 loops on hook; repeat from ★ 2 times **more**, YO and draw through all 4 loops on hook. Skip st **behind** FP Cluster unless otherwise indicated.

The Moose Chart, Square Two, and Panel Two were used to create the afghan on page 5.

Center Panel

Finished Size: 21" x 30¼" (53.5 cm x 77 cm)

Choose a chart from pages 25-28. Each block on the chart represents one hdc and the color indicates the Main Color and the Contrasting Color. Use separate balls for each section of the chart.

KEY

- Main Color

- Contrasting Color

To change colors, work the stitch **before** the color change to the last step (3 loops on hook), drop yarn, with new color, YO and draw through all loops on hook ***(Fig. A)***.
Drop old color to wrong side; cut yarn when it is no longer being used.

Fig. A

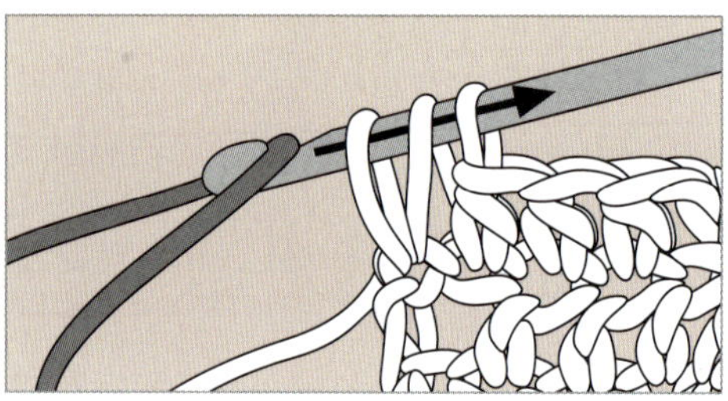

With smaller size hook and CC, ch 77, place marker in second ch from hook for Border placement.

Row 1 (Right side)**:** Hdc in third ch from hook **(2 skipped chs count as first hdc)** and in each ch across: 75 hdc.

Note: Loop a short piece of yarn around any stitch to mark Row 1 as **right** side **and** bottom edge.

Row 2: Ch 2 **(counts as first hdc, now and throughout Center Panel)**, turn; hdc in next hdc and in each hdc across.

Rows 3-91: Follow desired chart.

Finish off.

BORDER

Rnd 1: With **right** side of bottom edge facing, using larger size hook and working in free loops of beginning ch ***(Fig. 2b, page 30)***, join CC with slip st in first ch; ch 1, 2 sc in same st, work 68 sc evenly spaced across to marked ch, 2 sc in marked ch, remove marker; work 104 sc evenly spaced across end of rows; 2 sc in first hdc of Row 91, work 68 sc evenly spaced across to last hdc, 2 sc in last hdc; work 104 sc evenly spaced across end of rows; join with slip st to first sc: 352 sc.

Rnd 2: Slip st in next sc, [ch 2, working **around** first hdc, hdc in same st as joining **(beginning Cross St made)**], work Cross Sts around; join with slip st to first hdc changing to MC ***(Fig. B)***, drop CC: 176 Cross Sts.

Fig. B

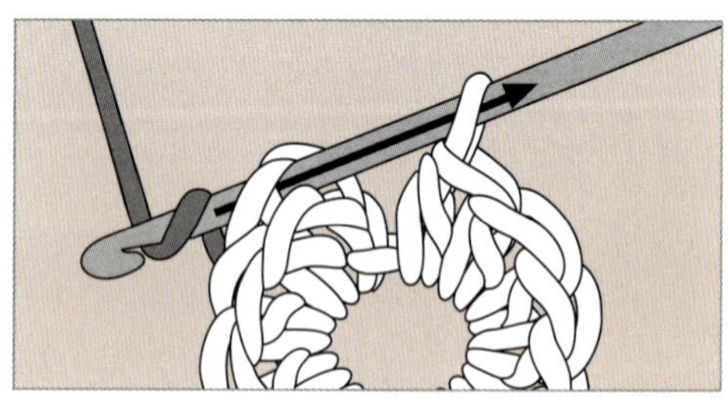

The Wolf Chart, Square Four, and Panel Three were used to create the afghan on page 7.

Rnd 3: With MC, slip st in next hdc, ch 2, † [hdc in sp **before** next hdc *(Fig. C)*, hdc in second hdc of next Cross St] 35 times, 4 hdc in sp **before** next hdc, hdc in second hdc of next Cross St, [hdc in sp **before** next hdc, hdc in second hdc of next Cross St] 51 times, 4 hdc in sp **before** next hdc †, hdc in second hdc of next Cross St, repeat from † to † once; join with slip st to first hdc changing to CC, drop MC: 364 hdc.

Fig. C

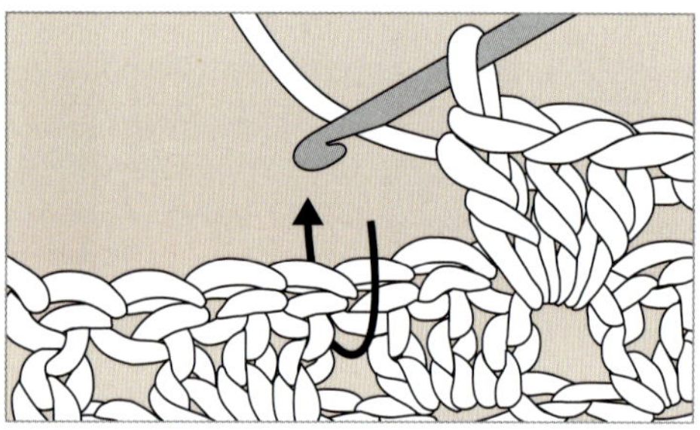

Rnd 4: [Ch 2, working **around** first, hdc in same st as joining **(beginning Cross St made)**], work Cross Sts around; join with slip st to first hdc changing to MC, cut CC: 182 Cross Sts.

Rnd 5: With MC, (slip st, ch 1, sc) in next hdc, sc in sp **before** next hdc, ★ sc in second hdc of next Cross St, sc in sp **before** next hdc; repeat from ★ around; join with slip st to first sc, finish off: 364 sc.

Corner Square (Make 4)

Choose a square on pages 10-15. You may make four of the same square, or mix-and-match the squares.

Side Panels

(Make 2 Short and 2 Long)

Choose a panel on pages 16-24. You may make them all using the same panel or mix-and-match.

Assembly

With MC and using mattress stitch *(Figs. 4a & b, page 31)*, sew Side Panels to Center Panel; then sew Corner Squares in place.

Edging

Rnd 1: With **right** side facing and larger size hook, join MC with slip st to any stitch on outer edge; ch 2 **(counts as first hdc)**, hdc in next st and in each st around working 4 hdc in each corner; join with slip st to first hdc.

Rnd 2: Ch 1, sc in same st as joining and in each hdc around; join with slip st to first sc.

Finish off **OR** do **not** finish off and work Optional Rnd 3.

Optional Rnd 3: Ch 1, working around Rnd 2, sc in each hdc on Rnd 1; join with slip st to first sc, finish off.

The Bear Chart, Square Three, and Panel Three were used to create the afghan on page 9.

Finished Size: 6¾" (17 cm) square

Square One

Rnd 1 (Right side)**:** With MC and using larger size hook, ch 2, 8 hdc in second ch from hook; join with slip st to first hdc.

Note: Loop a short piece of yarn around any stitch to mark Rnd 1 as **right** side.

Rnd 2: Ch 1 loosely, 2 hdc in same st as joining and in each hdc around; join with slip st to first hdc: 16 hdc.

Rnd 3: Ch 1 loosely, work FPdc around same st as joining and around next hdc, hdc in next hdc, (hdc, ch 1, hdc) in next hdc, ★ hdc in next hdc, work FPdc around post of same hdc worked into, work FPdc around next hdc, hdc in next hdc, (hdc, ch 1, hdc) in next hdc; repeat from ★ 2 times **more**, hdc in same hdc as first FPdc worked around; join with slip st to first FPdc: 24 sts and 4 ch-1 sps.

Rnd 4: Ch 1 loosely, skip same st as joining **(now and throughout)**, hdc in next 3 sts, (2 hdc, ch 1, 2 hdc) in next ch-1 sp, ★ skip next hdc, hdc in next 5 sts, (2 hdc, ch 1, 2 hdc) in next ch-1 sp; repeat from ★ 2 times **more**, skip next hdc, hdc in last hdc and in joining slip st; join with slip st to first hdc: 36 sts and 4 ch-1 sps.

Rnd 5: Ch 1 loosely, work FPtr around each of first 2 FPdc 2 rnds **below**, ★ † hdc in next 3 hdc, (2 hdc, ch 1, 2 hdc) in next ch-1 sp, skip next hdc †, hdc in next 3 hdc, work FPtr around each of next 2 FPdc 2 rnds **below**; repeat from ★ 2 times **more**, then repeat from † to † once, hdc in last 2 hdc and in joining slip st; join with slip st to first FPtr: 48 sts and 4 ch-1 sps.

Rnd 6: Ch 1 loosely, hdc in next 6 sts, (2 hdc, ch 1, 2 hdc) in next ch-1 sp, ★ skip next hdc, hdc in next 11 sts, (2 hdc, ch 1, 2 hdc) in next ch-1 sp; repeat from ★ 2 times **more**, skip next hdc, hdc in last 4 hdc and in joining slip st; join with slip st to first hdc: 60 hdc and 4 ch-1 sps.

Rnd 7: Ch 1 loosely, work FPtr around each of first 2 FPtr 2 rnds **below**, ★ † hdc in next hdc, work FPtr around hdc one rnd **below** each of next 2 hdc, hdc in next 3 hdc, (2 hdc, ch 1, 2 hdc) in next ch-1 sp, skip next hdc, hdc in next 3 hdc, work FPtr around hdc one rnd **below** each of next 2 hdc, hdc in next hdc †, work FPtr around each of next 2 FPtr 2 rnds **below**; repeat from ★ 2 times **more**, then repeat from † to † once; join with slip st to first FPtr: 72 sts and 4 ch-1 sps.

Corner Squares

Rnd 8: Ch 1 loosely, hdc in next 9 sts, (2 hdc, ch 1, 2 hdc) in next ch-1 sp, ★ skip next hdc, hdc in next 17 sts, (2 hdc, ch 1, 2 hdc) in next ch-1 sp; repeat from ★ 2 times **more**, skip next hdc, hdc in last 7 hdc and in joining slip st; join with slip st to first hdc: 84 hdc and 4 ch-1 sps.

Rnd 9: Ch 1 loosely, work FPtr around each of first 2 FPtr 2 rnds **below**, hdc in next hdc, work FPtr around each of next 2 FPtr 2 rnds **below**, hdc in next hdc, ★ † work FPtr around hdc one row **below** each of next 2 hdc, hdc in next 3 hdc, (2 hdc, ch 1, 2 hdc) in next ch-1 sp, skip next hdc, hdc in next 3 hdc, work FPtr around hdc one rnd **below** each of next 2 hdc, hdc in next hdc †, (work FPtr around each of next 2 FPtr 2 rnds **below**, hdc in next hdc) 3 times; repeat from ★ 2 times **more**, then repeat from † to † once, work FPtr around each of next 2 FPtr 2 rnds **below**, hdc in last hdc; join with slip st to first FPtr: 96 sts and 4 ch-1 sps.

Rnd 10: Ch 1 loosely, sc in next 12 sts, (sc, ch 1, sc) in next ch-1 sp, ★ skip next hdc, sc in next 23 sts, (sc, ch 1, sc) in next ch-1 sp; repeat from ★ 2 times **more**, skip next hdc, sc in last 10 sts and in joining slip st; join with slip st to first sc: 100 sc and 4 ch-1 sps.

Rnd 11: Ch 1 loosely, sc in next 12 sc, 3 sc in next ch-1 sp, ★ skip next sc, sc in next 24 sc, 3 sc in next ch-1 sp; repeat from ★ 2 times **more**, sc in last 11 sc and in joining slip st; join with slip st to first sc, finish off leaving a long end for sewing: 108 sc.

Square Two

Rnd 1 (Right side)**:** With MC and using larger size hook, ch 3, (2 dc, ch 1) 4 times in third ch from hook; join with slip st to first dc: 8 dc and 4 ch-1 sps.

Note: Loop a short piece of yarn around any stitch to mark Rnd 1 as **right** side.

Rnd 2: Ch 1 loosely, work BPdc around same st as joining and around next dc, (hdc, ch 1, hdc) in next ch-1 sp, ★ work BPdc around each of next 2 dc, (hdc, ch 1, hdc) in next ch-1 sp; repeat from ★ 2 times **more**; join with slip st to first BPdc: 16 sts and 4 ch-1 sps.

Rnd 3: Ch 1 loosely, work BPdc around same st as joining and around each of next 2 sts, (2 hdc, ch 1, 2 hdc) in next ch-1 sp, ★ work BPdc around each of next 4 sts, (2 hdc, ch 1, 2 hdc) in next ch-1 sp; repeat from ★ 2 times **more**, work BPdc around last st; join with slip st to first BPdc: 32 sts and 4 ch-1 sps.

Rnd 4: Ch 1 loosely, work BPdc around same st as joining and around each of next 4 sts, (2 hdc, ch 1, 2 hdc) in next ch-1 sp, ★ work BPdc around each of next 8 sts, (2 hdc, ch 1, 2 hdc) in next ch-1 sp; repeat from ★ 2 times **more**, work BPdc around each of last 3 sts; join with slip st to first BPdc: 48 sts and 4 ch-1 sps.

Rnd 5: Ch 1 loosely, work BPdc around same st as joining and around each of next 6 sts, (2 hdc, ch 1, 2 hdc) in next ch-1 sp, ★ work BPdc around each of next 12 sts, (2 hdc, ch 1, 2 hdc) in next ch-1 sp; repeat from ★ 2 times **more**, work BPdc around each of last 5 sts; join with slip st to first BPdc: 64 sts and 4 ch-1 sps.

Rnd 6: Ch 1 loosely, work BPdc around same st as joining and around each of next 8 sts, 2 sc in next ch-1 sp, ★ work BPdc around each of next 16 sts, 2 sc in next ch-1 sp; repeat from ★ 2 times **more**, work BPdc around each of last 7 sts; join with slip st to first BPdc: 72 sts.

Rnd 7: Ch 2 loosely, tr in same st as joining, ★ † dc in next 3 sts, hdc in next 2 sts, sc in next 2 sts, slip st in next 2 sc, sc in next 2 sts, hdc in next 2 sts, dc in next 3 sts †, tr in next 2 sts; repeat from ★ 2 times **more**, then repeat from † to † once, tr in last st; join with slip st to first tr.

Rnd 8: Ch 1 loosely, (2 dc, ch 1, 2 dc) in same st as joining, ★ † dc in next 2 sts, hdc in next 4 sts, sc in next st, slip st in next 3 sts, sc in next st, hdc in next 4 sts, dc in next 2 sts †, (2 dc, ch 1, 2 dc) in next st; repeat from ★ 2 times **more**, then repeat from † to † once; join with slip st to first dc: 84 sts and 4 ch-1 sps.

Rnd 9: Ch 1 loosely, hdc in next st, ★ † (hdc, ch 1, hdc) in next ch-1 sp, skip next st, hdc in next 6 sts, sc in next 8 sts †, hdc in next 6 sts; repeat from ★ 2 times **more**, then repeat from † to † once, hdc in last 4 sts and in joining slip st; join with slip st to first hdc: 88 sts and 4 ch-1 sps.

Rnd 10: Ch 1, sc in same st as joining and in next hdc, 5 sc in next ch-1 sp, ★ skip next st, sc in next 21 sts, 5 sc in next ch-1 sp; repeat from ★ 2 times **more**, skip next st, sc in last 19 sts; join with slip st to first sc, finish off leaving a long end for sewing: 104 sc.

Square Three

Rnd 1 (Right side)**:** With MC and using larger size hook, ch 2, 8 sc in second ch from hook; join with slip st to first sc.

Note: Loop a short piece of yarn around any stitch to mark Rnd 1 as **right** side.

Rnd 2: Ch 1, 2 sc in same st as joining and in each sc around; join with slip st to first sc: 16 sc.

Rnd 3: Ch 2 **(counts as first hdc, now and throughout)**, hdc in same st as joining and in next sc, (2 hdc in next sc, hdc in next sc) around; join with slip st to first hdc: 24 hdc.

Rnd 4: Ch 1 loosely, work FP Cluster around same st as joining, hdc in next hdc, (work FP Cluster around next hdc, hdc in next hdc) around; join with slip st to first FP Cluster: 12 FP Clusters and 12 hdc.

Rnd 5: Ch 1, 2 sc in same st as joining and in each st around; join with slip st to first sc: 48 sc.

Rnd 6: Ch 2, hdc in same st as joining and in next 7 sc, (2 hdc in next sc, hdc in next 7 sc) around; join with slip st to first hdc: 54 hdc.

Rnd 7: Ch 2, hdc in same st as joining and in next 8 hdc, (2 hdc in next hdc, hdc in next 8 hdc) around; join with slip st to first hdc: 60 hdc.

Rnd 8: Ch 1 loosely, work FP Cluster around same st as joining, hdc in next hdc, (work FP Cluster around next hdc, hdc in next hdc) around; join with slip st to first FP Cluster: 30 FP Clusters and 30 hdc.

Rnd 9: Ch 1, 2 sc in same st as joining, sc in next 4 sts, (2 sc in next st, sc in next 4 sts) around; join with slip st to first sc: 72 sc.

Rnd 10: Ch 1, sc in same st as joining and in next 3 sc, ★ † hdc in next 2 sc, dc in next 2 sc, (dc, 2 tr) in next sc, (2 tr, dc) in next sc, dc in next 2 sc, hdc in next 2 sc †, sc in next 8 sc; repeat from ★ 2 times **more**, then repeat from † to † once, sc in last 4 sc; join with slip st to first sc: 88 sts.

Rnd 11: Ch 1, sc in same st as joining and in next 10 sts, 3 sc in next st, (sc in next 21 sts, 3 sc in next st) 3 times, sc in last 10 sts; join with slip st to first sc: 96 sc.

Rnd 12: Ch 1, sc in same st as joining and in next 11 sc, 3 sc in next sc, (sc in next 23 sc, 3 sc in next sc) 3 times, sc in last 11 sc; join with slip st to first sc, finish off leaving a long end for sewing: 104 sc.

Square Four

Rnd 1 (Right side)**:** With MC and using larger size hook, ch 2, 8 sc in second ch from hook; join with slip st to first sc.

Note: Loop a short piece of yarn around any stitch to mark Rnd 1 as **right** side.

Rnd 2: Ch 2 **(counts as first hdc, now and throughout)**, hdc in same st as joining, 2 hdc in each sc around; join with slip st to first hdc: 16 hdc.

Rnd 3: Ch 2, hdc in next hdc, work FPdc around hdc just worked into, ★ hdc in next 2 hdc, work FPdc around last hdc worked into; repeat from ★ around; join with slip st to first hdc: 24 sts.

Rnd 4: Ch 2, hdc in same st as joining and in next 2 sts, (2 hdc in next st, hdc in next 2 sts) around; join with slip st to first hdc: 32 sts.

Rnd 5: Ch 2, work FPtr around last FPdc made on Rnd 3, work FPtr around next FPdc 2 rnds **below**, do **not** skip sts behind either FPtr, ★ hdc in next 4 sts, work FPtr around same FPdc on Rnd 3 as last FPtr (working **above** last FPtr made), work FPtr around next FPdc 2 rnds **below**; repeat from ★ around to last 3 hdc, hdc in last 3 hdc; join with slip st to first hdc: 48 sts.

Rnd 6: Ch 1, sc in same st as joining and in each sc around; join with slip st to first sc.

Rnd 7: Ch 1, slip st in Front Loop Only of each sc around ***(Fig. 1, page 30)***; join with slip st to Back Loop Only of first slip st.

Rnd 8: Ch 1, working in free loops on Rnd 6 ***(Fig. 2a, page 30)***, sc in each st around; join with slip st to **both** loops of first sc.

Rnd 9: Ch 1, sc in same st as joining and in next 2 sc, work FPdc around last sc worked into, ★ sc in next 3 sc, work FPdc around last sc worked into; repeat from ★ around; join with slip st to first sc: 64 sts.

Rnd 10: Ch 2, hdc in next st and in each st around; join with slip st to first hdc.

Rnd 11: Ch 1, work FPtr around last FPdc made on Rnd 9, work FPtr around next FPdc 2 rnds **below**, skip next st behind post sts, hdc in next 3 hdc, ★ work FPtr around same FPdc on Rnd 9 as last FPtr (working **above** last FPtr made), work FPtr around next FPdc 2 rnds **below**, skip next st behind post sts, hdc in next 3 hdc; repeat from ★ around working last hdc in joining slip st; join with slip st to first FPtr: 80 sts.

Rnd 12: Ch 1, sc in same st as joining and in each st around; join with slip st to first sc.

Rnd 13: Ch 1, sc in same st as joining and in next 3 sc, ★ † hdc in next 2 sc, dc in next sc, 2 dc in each of next 2 sc, dc in next sc, hdc in next 2 sc, sc in next 4 sc, slip st in next 4 sc †, sc in next 4 sc; repeat from ★ 2 times **more**, then repeat from † to † once; join with slip st to first sc: 88 sts.

Rnd 14: Ch 1, sc in same st as joining and in next 3 sc, ★ † work BPdc around each of next 3 sts, 2 BPdc around each of next 2 sts, work BPdc around each of next 3 sts †, sc in next 14 sts (working **around** 4 slip sts on Rnd 13 into sc on Rnd 12); repeat from ★ 2 times **more**, then repeat from † to † once, sc in last 10 sts (working **around** 4 slip sts on Rnd 13 into sc on Rnd 12); join with slip st to first sc, finish off leaving a long end for sewing: 96 sts.

SIZE INFORMATION

Finished Width: 6¾" (17 cm)

Finished Length:

21{30¼}"/53.5{77} cm

Size Note: We have printed the instructions for the length of the Panels in different colors to make it easier for you to find:

- Short Panel in Blue
- Long Panel in Pink

Instructions in Black apply to both lengths.

Panel One

With MC and using larger size hook, ch 26.

Row 1 (Right side)**:** Sc in second ch from hook and in each ch across: 25 sc.

Note: Loop a short piece of yarn around any stitch to mark Row 1 as **right** side.

Row 2: Ch 2 **(counts as first hdc, now and throughout)**, turn; hdc in first sc and in each sc across: 26 hdc.

Side Panels

Row 3: Ch 2, turn; hdc in next hdc, work FPdc around each of next 2 hdc, ★ hdc in next hdc, work FPdc around next hdc, hdc in next 4 hdc, work FPdc around next hdc, hdc in next hdc, work FPdc around each of next 2 hdc; repeat from ★ once **more**, hdc in last 2 hdc.

Row 4 AND ALL WRONG SIDE ROWS: Ch 2, turn; hdc in next hdc and in each st across.

Row 5: Ch 2, turn; hdc in next hdc, work FPtr around each of next 2 FPdc 2 rows **below**, ★ hdc in next hdc, work FPtr around next FPdc 2 rows **below**, hdc in next 4 hdc, work FPtr around next FPdc 2 rows **below**, hdc in next hdc, work FPtr around each of next 2 FPdc 2 rows **below**; repeat from ★ once **more**, hdc in last 2 hdc.

Row 7: Ch 2, turn; hdc in next hdc, work FPtr around each of next 2 FPtr 2 rows **below**, hdc in next 2 hdc, ★ (work FPtr around next FPtr 2 rows **below**, hdc in next 2 hdc) twice, work FPtr around each of next 2 FPtr 2 rows **below**, hdc in next 2 hdc; repeat from ★ once **more**.

Row 9: Ch 2, turn; hdc in next hdc, work FPtr around each of next 2 FPtr 2 rows **below**, (hdc in next 3 hdc, work FPtr around each of next 2 FPtr 2 rows **below**) across to last 2 hdc, hdc in last 2 hdc.

Row 11: Ch 2, turn; hdc in next hdc, work FPtr around each of next 2 FPtr 2 rows **below**, hdc in next 2 hdc, ★ skip next FPtr 2 rows **below**, work FPtr around next FPtr, hdc in next 2 hdc, working in **front** of last FPtr made, work FPtr around skipped FPtr 2 rows **below**, hdc in next 2 hdc, work FPtr around each of next 2 FPtr 2 rows **below**, hdc in next 2 hdc; repeat from ★ once **more**.

Row 13: Ch 2, turn; hdc in next hdc, work FPtr around each of next 2 FPtr 2 rows **below**, ★ hdc in next hdc, work FPtr around next FPtr 2 rows **below**, hdc in next 4 hdc, work FPtr around next FPtr 2 rows **below**, hdc in next hdc, work FPtr around each of next 2 FPtr 2 rows **below**; repeat from ★ once **more**, hdc in last 2 hdc.

Row 15: Ch 2, turn; hdc in next hdc, work FPtr around each of next 2 FPtr 2 rows **below**, ★ hdc in next hdc, work FPtr around next FPtr 2 rows **below**, hdc in next 4 hdc, work FPtr around next FPtr 2 rows **below**, hdc in next hdc, work FPtr around each of next 2 FPtr 2 rows **below**; repeat from ★ once **more**, hdc in last 2 hdc.

Row 16: Ch 2, turn; hdc in next hdc and in each st across.

Rows 17 thru 68{98}: Repeat Rows 7-16, 5{8} times; then repeat Rows 15 and 16 once.

Border Rnd: Ch 1, turn; 2 sc in first hdc, sc in next 11 hdc, sc2tog, sc in next 11 hdc, 2 sc in last hdc; work 75{107} sc evenly spaced across end of rows; working in free loops of beginning ch ***(Fig. 2b, page 30)***, 2 sc in first ch, sc in next 23 chs, 2 sc in next ch; work 75{107} sc evenly spaced across end of rows; join with slip st to first sc, finish off.

Panel Two

With MC and using larger size hook, ch 26.

Row 1 (Right side)**:** Sc in second ch from hook and in each ch across: 25 sc.

Note: Loop a short piece of yarn around any stitch to mark Row 1 as **right** side.

Row 2: Ch 2 **(counts as first hdc, now and throughout)**, turn; hdc in first sc and in each sc across: 26 hdc.

Row 3: Ch 2, turn; hdc in next hdc, work FPdc around each of next 2 hdc, hdc in next 6 hdc, work FPdc around each of next 2 hdc, hdc in next 5 hdc, work FPdc around each of next 4 hdc, hdc in last 5 hdc.

Row 4 AND ALL WRONG SIDE ROWS: Ch 2, turn; hdc in next hdc and in each st across.

Row 5: Ch 2, hdc in next hdc, work FPtr around each of next 2 FPdc 2 rows **below**, hdc in next 6 hdc, work FPtr around each of next 2 FPdc 2 rows **below**, hdc in next 4 hdc, work FPtr around each of next 2 FPdc 2 rows **below**, hdc in next 2 hdc, work FPtr around each of next 2 FPdc 2 rows **below**, hdc in last 4 hdc.

Row 7: Ch 2, turn; hdc in next 2 hdc, work FPtr around each of next 2 FPtr 2 rows **below**, ★ hdc in next 4 hdc, work FPtr around each of next 2 FPtr 2 rows **below**; repeat from ★ 2 times **more**, hdc in last 3 hdc.

Row 9: Ch 2, turn; hdc in next 3 hdc, work FPtr around each of next 2 FPtr 2 rows **below**, hdc in next 2 hdc, work FPtr around each of next 2 FPtr 2 rows **below**, hdc in next 4 hdc, work FPtr around each of next 2 FPtr 2 rows **below**, hdc in next 6 hdc, work FPtr around each of next 2 FPtr 2 rows **below**, hdc in last 2 hdc.

Row 11: Ch 2, turn; hdc in next hdc, work FPtr around hdc one row **below** each of next 2 hdc, hdc in next hdc, work FPtr around each of next 4 FPtr 2 rows **below**, hdc in next hdc, work FPtr around hdc one row **below** each of next 2 hdc, hdc in next 2 hdc, work FPtr around each of next 2 FPtr 2 rows **below**, hdc in next hdc, work FPtr around hdc one row **below** each of next 4 hdc, hdc in next hdc, work FPtr around each of next 2 FPtr 2 rows **below**, hdc in last 2 hdc.

Row 13: Ch 2, turn; hdc in next hdc, work FPtr around each of next 2 FPtr 2 rows **below**, hdc in next hdc, work FPtr around each of next 4 FPtr 2 rows **below**, hdc in next hdc, work FPtr around each of next 2 FPtr 2 rows **below**, hdc in next 2 hdc, work FPtr around each of next 2 FPtr 2 rows **below**, hdc in next hdc, work FPtr around each of next 4 FPtr 2 rows **below**, hdc in next hdc, work FPtr around each of next 2 FPtr 2 rows **below**, hdc in last 2 hdc.

Row 15: Ch 2, turn; hdc in next hdc, work FPtr around each of next 2 FPtr 2 rows **below**, hdc in next 6 hdc, skip next 4 FPtr 2 rows **below**, work FPtr around each of next 2 FPtr 2 rows **below**, hdc in next 4 hdc, skip next 2 FPtr 2 rows **below,** work FPtr around each of next 2 FPtr 2 rows **below**, hdc in next 2 hdc, work FPtr around each of next 2 FPtr 2 rows **below**, hdc in last 4 hdc.

Row 16: Ch 2, turn; hdc in next hdc and in each st across.

Rows 17 thru 60{90}: Repeat Rows 7-16, 4{7} times; then repeat Rows 7-10 once **more**.

Row 61{91}: Ch 2, turn; hdc in next 4 hdc, work FPtr around each of next 4 FPtr 2 rows **below**, hdc in next 5 hdc, work FPtr around each of next 2 FPtr 2 rows **below**, hdc in next 6 hdc, work FPtr around each of next 2 FPtr 2 rows **below**, hdc in last 2 hdc.

Row 62{92}: Ch 2, turn; hdc in next st and in each st across.

Last 2 Rows: Repeat Rows 61 and 62 {91 and 92}.

Border Rnd: Ch 1, turn; 2 sc in first hdc, sc in next 11 hdc, sc2tog, sc in next 11 hdc, 2 sc in last hdc; work 75{107} sc evenly spaced across end of rows; working in free loops of beginning ch ***(Fig. 2b, page 30)***, 2 sc in first ch, sc in next 23 chs, 2 sc in next ch; work 75{107} sc evenly spaced across end of rows; join with slip st to first sc, finish off.

Panel Three

With MC and using larger size hook, ch 26.

Row 1: Sc in second ch from hook and in each ch across: 25 sc.

Row 2 (Right side)**:** Ch 2 **(does not count as a st, now and throughout)**, turn; hdc in first 6 sc, ch 1, skip next sc, hdc in next 11 sc, ch 1, skip next sc, hdc in last 6 sc: 23 hdc and 2 ch-1 sps.

Note: Loop a short piece of yarn around any stitch to mark Row 2 as **right** side.

Row 3: Ch 2, turn; hdc in first 6 hdc, ch 1, skip next ch-1 sp, hdc in next 11 hdc, ch 1, skip next ch-1 sp, hdc in last 6 hdc.

Row 4: Ch 2, turn; hdc in first 2 hdc, † ch 6, skip next 4 hdc, working in **front** of Row 3, slip st in ch-1 sp one row **below** next ch-1 sp (on Row 2), ch 6, skip next 4 hdc on Row 3 †, hdc in next 3 hdc, repeat from † to † once, hdc in last 2 hdc: 7 hdc and 4 ch-6 sps.

Row 5: Ch 1, turn; sc in first 2 hdc, † working in **front** of next ch-6, dc in next 2 hdc on Row 3, 2 dc in next hdc, ch 1, skip next ch-1 sp, dc in next 4 hdc †, sc in next 3 hdc on Row 4, repeat from † to † once, sc in last 2 hdc on Row 3: 23 sts and 2 ch-1 sps.

Row 6: Ch 2, turn; hdc in first 2 sc, † ch 6, skip next 4 dc, working in **front** of previous row, slip st in ch-1 sp one row **below** next ch-1 sp, ch 6, skip next 4 dc on previous row †, hdc in next 3 sc, repeat from † to † once, hdc in last 2 sc: 7 hdc and 4 ch-6 sps.

Row 7: Ch 1, turn; sc in first 2 hdc, † working in **front** of **and** in row **below** next ch-6, dc in next 4 dc, ch 1, skip next ch-1 sp, dc in next 4 dc †, sc in next 3 hdc on previous row, repeat from † to † once, sc in last 2 hdc on previous row: 23 sts and 2 ch-1 sps.

Rows 8 thru 72{106}: Repeat Rows 6 and 7, 32{49} times; then repeat Row 6 once **more**: 7 hdc and 4 ch-6 sps.

Row 73{107}: Ch 1, turn; sc in first 2 hdc, † working in **front** of **and** in row **below** next ch-6, dc in next 4 dc, dc in next ch-1 sp and in next 4 dc †, sc in next 3 hdc on previous row, repeat from † to † once, sc in last 2 hdc on previous row: 25 sts.

Row 74{108}: Ch 2, turn; hdc in each st across.

Row 75{109}: Ch 1, turn; sc in each hdc across.

Border Rnd: Ch 1, turn; 2 sc in first hdc, sc in next 23 hdc, 2 sc in last hdc; work 75{107} sc evenly spaced across end of rows; working in free loops of beginning ch ***(Fig. 2b, page 30)***, 2 sc in first ch, sc in next 23 chs, 2 sc in next ch; work 75{107} sc evenly spaced across end of rows; join with slip st to first sc, finish off.

Panel Four

With MC and using larger size hook, ch 26.

Row 1 (Right side)**:** Sc in second ch from hook and in each ch across: 25 sc.

Note: Loop a short piece of yarn around any stitch to mark Row 1 as **right** side.

Row 2: Ch 2 **(does not count as a st, now and throughout)**, turn; hdc in first sc and in each sc across.

Row 3: Ch 2, turn; hdc in first hdc, † skip next hdc, work FP Cluster around next hdc, hdc in same hdc just worked around and in next hdc, skip next hdc, work FP Cluster around next hdc †, hdc in same hdc just worked around and in next 4 hdc, work FPdc around each of next 4 hdc, hdc in next 4 hdc, repeat from † to † once, hdc in same hdc just worked around and in last 2 hdc.

Row 4: Ch 2, turn; hdc in first 10 sts, work BPdc around each of next 4 FPdc, skip next 4 sts from last hdc made, hdc in last 11 sts.

Row 5: Ch 2, turn; hdc in first hdc, † work FP Cluster around hdc **after** FP Cluster 2 rows **below**, skip next hdc from last hdc made, hdc in next 2 sts, work FP Cluster around hdc **after** FP Cluster 2 rows **below**, skip next st from last hdc made †, hdc in next 4 sts, work FPdc around each of next 2 BPdc, skip next 2 sts from last hdc made, hdc in next 2 sts, work FPdc around each of next 2 BPdc, skip next 2 sts from last hdc made, hdc in next 3 sts, repeat from † to † once, hdc in last 3 sts.

Row 6: Ch 2, turn; hdc in first 9 sts, work BPdc around each of next 2 FPdc, skip next 2 sts from last hdc made, hdc in next 2 sts, work BPdc around each of next 2 FPdc, skip next 2 sts from last hdc made, hdc in last 10 sts.

Row 7: Ch 2, turn; hdc in first hdc, † work FP Cluster around hdc **after** FP Cluster 2 rows **below**, skip next st from last hdc made, hdc in next 2 sts, work FP Cluster around hdc **after** FP Cluster 2 rows **below**, skip next hdc from last hdc made, hdc in next 3 sts †, work FPdc around each of next 2 BPdc, skip next 2 sts from last hdc made, hdc in next 4 sts, work FPdc around each of next 2 BPdc, skip next 2 sts from last hdc made, hdc in next 2 sts, repeat from † to † once.

Row 8: Ch 2, turn; hdc in first 8 sts, work BPdc around each of next 2 FPdc, skip next 2 sts from last hdc made, hdc in next 4 sts, work BPdc around each of next 2 FPdc, skip next 2 sts from last hdc made, hdc in last 9 sts.

Row 9: Ch 2, turn; hdc in first hdc, † work FP Cluster around hdc **after** FP Cluster 2 rows **below**, skip next st from last hdc made, hdc in next 2 sts, work FP Cluster around hdc **after** FP Cluster 2 rows **below**, skip next st from last hdc made †, hdc in next 2 sts, work FPdc around each of next 2 BPdc, skip next 2 sts from last hdc made, hdc in next 6 sts, work FPdc around each of next 2 BPdc, skip next 2 sts from last hdc made, hdc in next hdc, repeat from † to † once, hdc in last 3 sts.

Row 10: Ch 2, turn; hdc in first 7 sts, work BPdc around each of next 2 FPdc, skip next 2 sts from last hdc made, hdc in next 6 sts, work BPdc around each of next 2 FPdc, skip next 2 sts from last hdc made, hdc in last 8 sts.

Row 11: Ch 2, turn; hdc in first hdc, † work FP Cluster around hdc **after** FP Cluster 2 rows **below**, skip next st from last hdc made, hdc in next 2 sts, work FP Cluster around hdc **after** FP Cluster 2 rows **below**, skip next st from last hdc made †, hdc in next 2 sts, work FPdc around each of next 2 BPdc, skip next 2 sts from last hdc made, hdc in next 6 sts, work FPdc around each of next 2 BPdc, skip next 2 sts from last hdc made, hdc in next st, repeat from † to † once, hdc in last 3 sts.

Row 12: Ch 2, turn; hdc in first 7 sts, work BPdc around each of next 2 FPdc, skip next 2 sts from last hdc made, hdc in next 6 sts, work BPdc around each of next 2 FPdc, skip next 2 sts from last hdc made, hdc in last 8 sts.

Row 13: Ch 2, turn; hdc in first hdc, † work FP Cluster around hdc **after** FP Cluster 2 rows **below**, skip next st from last hdc made, hdc in next 2 hdc, work FP Cluster around hdc **after** FP Cluster 2 rows **below**, skip next st from last hdc made, hdc in next 3 sts †, work FPdc around each of next 2 BPdc, skip next 2 sts from last hdc made, hdc in next 4 sts, work FPdc around each of next 2 BPdc, skip next 2 sts from last hdc made, hdc in next 2 sts, repeat from † to † once.

Row 14: Ch 2, turn; hdc in first 8 sts, work BPdc around each of next 2 FPdc, skip next 2 sts from last hdc made, hdc in next 4 sts, work BPdc around each of next 2 FPdc, skip next 2 sts from last hdc made, hdc in last 9 sts.

Row 15: Ch 2, turn; hdc in first hdc, † work FP Cluster around hdc **after** FP Cluster 2 rows **below**, skip next st from last hdc made, hdc in next 2 sts, work FP Cluster around hdc **after** FP Cluster 2 rows **below**, skip next st from last hdc made †, hdc in next 4 sts, work FPdc around each of next 2 BPdc, skip next 2 sts from last hdc made, hdc in next 2 sts, work FPdc around each of next 2 BPdc, skip next 2 sts from last hdc made, hdc in next 3 sts, repeat from † to † once, hdc in last 3 sts.

Row 16: Ch 2, turn; hdc in first 9 sts, work BPdc around each of next 2 FPdc, skip next 2 sts from last hdc made, hdc in next 2 sts, work BPdc around each of next 2 FPdc, skip next 2 sts from last hdc made, hdc in last 10 sts.

Row 17: Ch 2, turn; hdc in first hdc, † work FP Cluster around hdc **after** FP Cluster 2 rows **below**, skip next st from last hdc made, hdc in next 2 hdc, work FP Cluster around hdc **after** FP Cluster 2 rows **below**, skip next st from last hdc made †, hdc in next 5 sts, work FPdc around each of next 4 BPdc, skip next 4 sts from last hdc made, hdc in next 4 sts, repeat from † to † once, hdc in last 3 sts.

Row 18: Ch 2, turn; hdc in first 10 sts, work BPdc around each of next 4 FPdc, skip next 4 sts from last hdc made, hdc in last 11 hdc.

Row 19: Ch 2, turn; hdc in first hdc, † work FP Cluster around hdc **after** FP Cluster 2 rows **below**, skip next st from last hdc made, hdc in next 2 sts, work FP Cluster around hdc **after** FP Cluster 2 rows **below**, skip next st from last hdc made †, hdc in next 5 sts, work FPdc around each of next 4 BPdc, skip next 4 sts from last hdc made, hdc in next 4 sts, repeat from † to † once, hdc in last 3 sts.

Rows 20 thru 66{98}: Repeat Rows 4-19, 2{4} times; then repeat Rows 4-18 once **more**.

Row 67{99}: Ch 1, turn; sc in each st across: 25 sts.

Border Rnd: Ch 1, do **not** turn; work 75{107} sc evenly spaced across end of rows; working in free loops of beginning ch *(Fig. 2b, page 30)*, 2 sc in first ch, sc in next 23 chs, 2 sc in next ch; work 75{107} sc evenly spaced across end of rows; working in sts across last row, 2 sc in first sc, sc in next 23 sc, 2 sc in last sc; join with slip st to first sc, finish off.

Charts

Bear

On **right** side rows, work chart from **right** to **left**; on **wrong** side rows, work chart from **left** to **right**.

KEY

- Main Color
- Contrasting Color

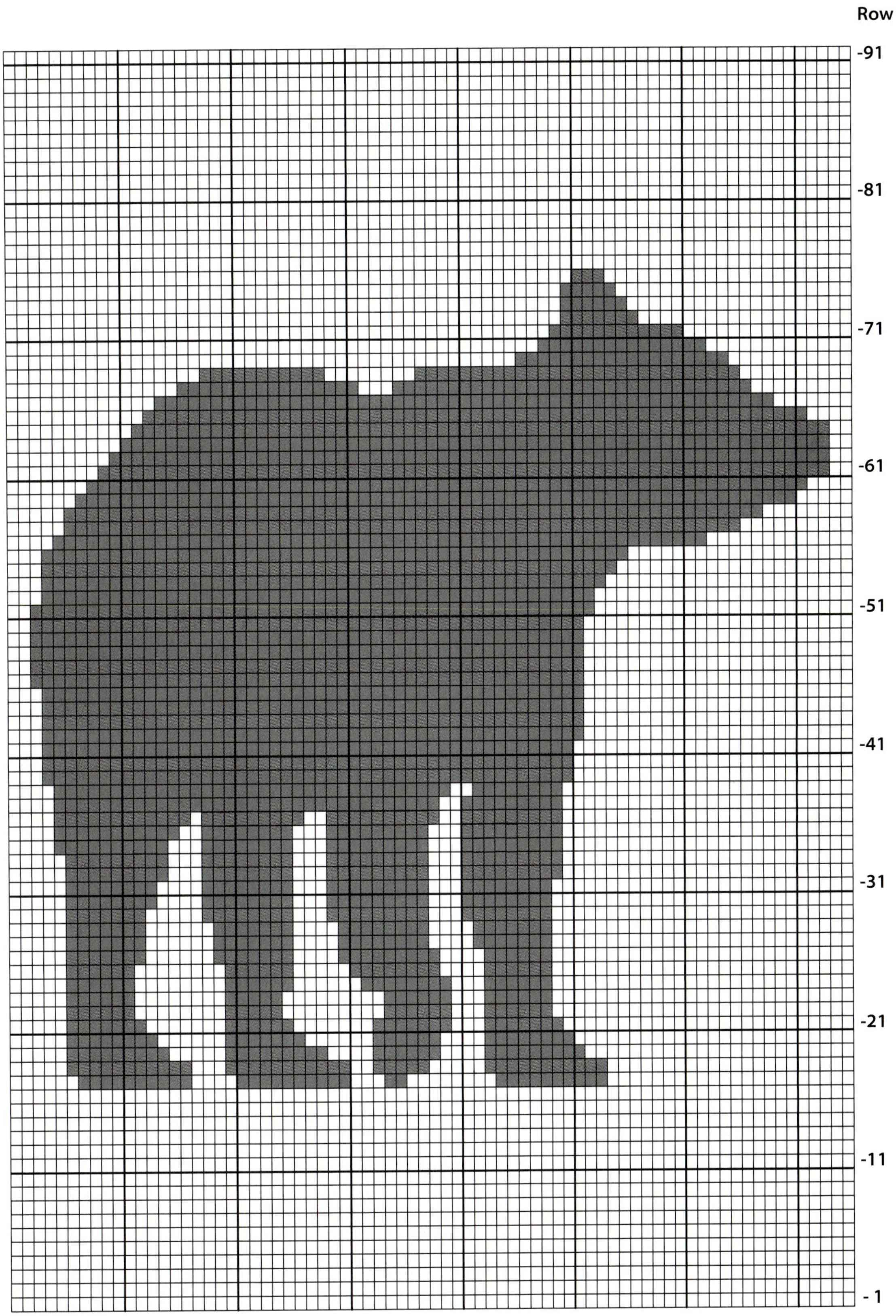

Wolf

On **right** side rows, work chart from **right** to **left**;

on **wrong** side rows, work chart from **left** to **right**.

KEY

- Main Color
- Contrasting Color

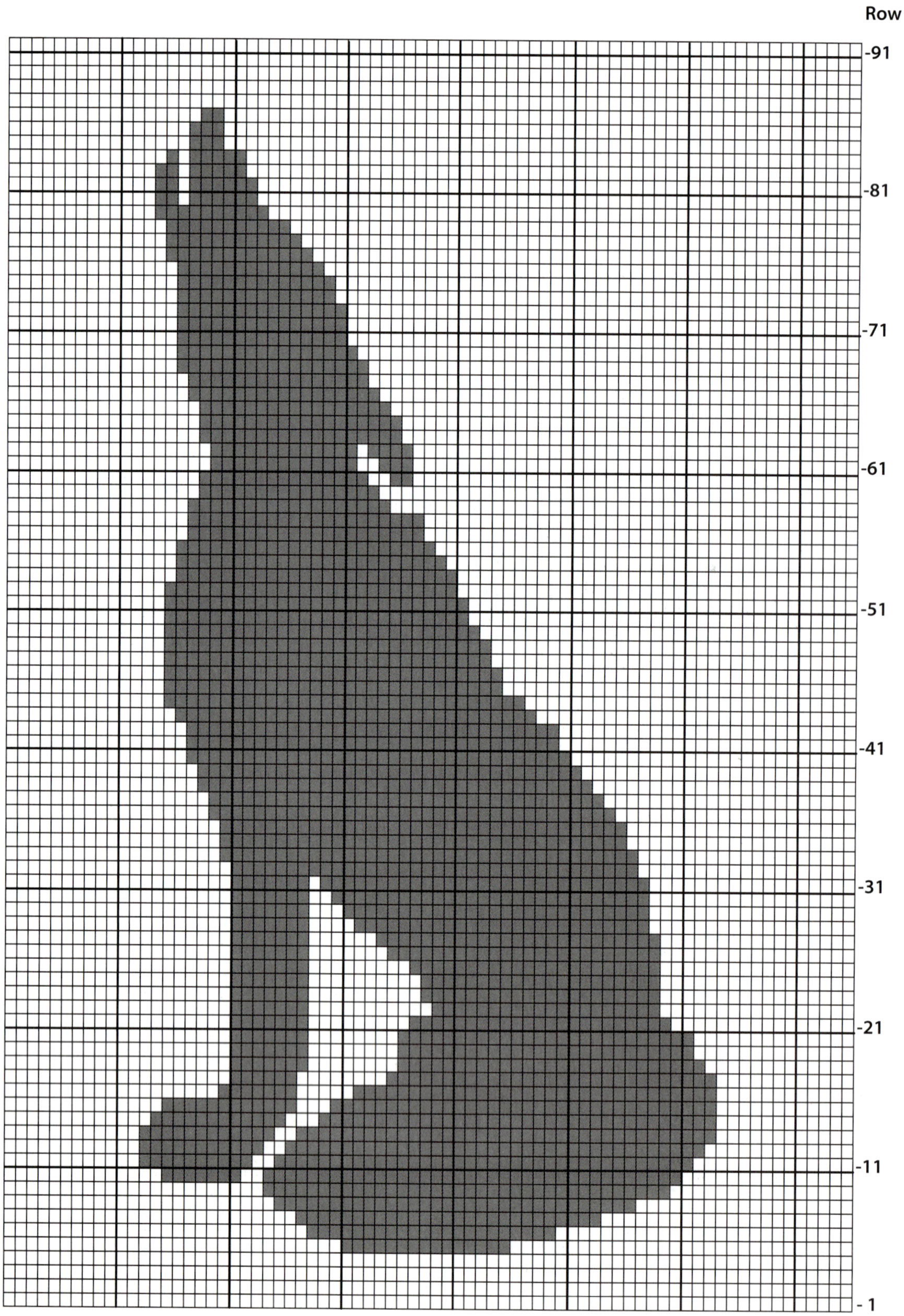

Moose

On **right** side rows, work chart from **right** to **left**;
on **wrong** side rows, work chart from **left** to **right**.

KEY

- Main Color

- Contrasting Color

Deer

On **right** side rows, work chart from **right** to **left**; on **wrong** side rows, work chart from **left** to **right**.

KEY

- Main Color

- Contrasting Color

General Instructions

ABBREVIATIONS

BPdc	Back Post double crochet(s)
CC	Contrasting Color
ch(s)	chain(s)
cm	centimeters
dc	double crochet(s)
FP	Front Post
FPdc	Front Post double crochet(s)
FPst(s)	Front Post stitch(es)
FPtr	Front Post treble crochet(s)
hdc	half double crochet(s)
MC	Main Color
Rnd(s)	Round(s)
sc	single crochet(s)
sc2tog	single crochet 2 together
sp(s)	space(s)
st(s)	stitch(es)
tr	treble crochet(s)
YO	yarn over

SYMBOLS & TERMS

★ — work instructions following ★ as many **more** times as indicated in addition to the first time.

† to † — work all instructions from first † to second † **as many** times as specified.

( ) or [ ] — work enclosed instructions **as many** times as specified by the number immediately following **or** work all enclosed instructions in the stitch or space indicated **or** contains explanatory remarks.

colon (:) — the number(s) given after a colon at the end of a row or round denote(s) the number of stitches or spaces you should have on that row or round.

CROCHET HOOKS																	
U.S.	B-1	C-2	D-3	E-4	F-5	G-6	7	H-8	I-9	J-10	K-10½	L-11	M/N-13	N/P-15	P/Q	Q	S
Metric - mm	2.25	2.75	3.25	3.5	3.75	4	4.5	5	5.5	6	6.5	8	9	10	15	16	19

BEGINNER	Projects for first-time crocheters using basic stitches. Minimal shaping.
EASY	Projects using yarn with basic stitches, repetitive stitch patterns, simple color changes, and simple shaping and finishing.
INTERMEDIATE	Projects using a variety of techniques, such as basic lace patterns or color patterns, mid-level shaping and finishing.
EXPERIENCED	Projects with intricate stitch patterns, techniques and dimension, such as non-repeating patterns, multi-color techniques, fine threads, small hooks, detailed shaping and refined finishing.

GAUGE

Exact gauge is essential for proper size. Before beginning your project, make the sample swatch given in the individual instructions in the yarn and hook specified. After completing the swatch, measure it, counting your stitches and rows carefully. If your swatch is larger or smaller than specified, **make another, changing hook size to get the correct gauge**. Keep trying until you find the size hook that will give you the specified gauge.

BACK OR FRONT LOOP ONLY

Work only in loop(s) indicated by arrow ***(Fig. 1)***.

Fig. 1

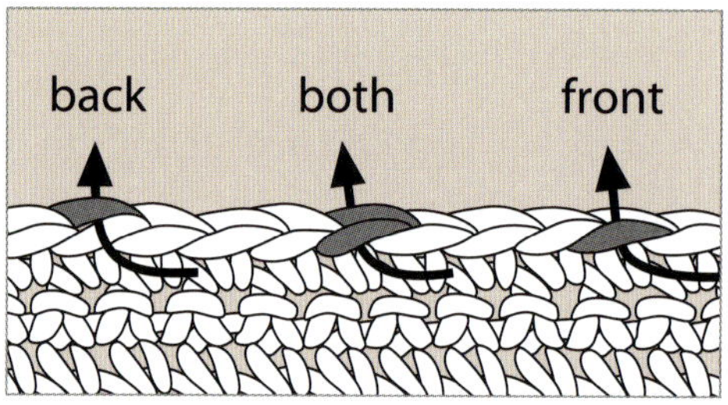

FREE LOOPS

After working in Back or Front Loops Only on a row or round, there will be a ridge of unused loops. These are called the free loops. Later, when instructed to work in the free loops of the same row or round, work in these loops ***(Fig. 2a)***.

When instructed to work in free loops of a chain, work in loop indicated by arrow ***(Fig. 2b)***.

Fig. 2a

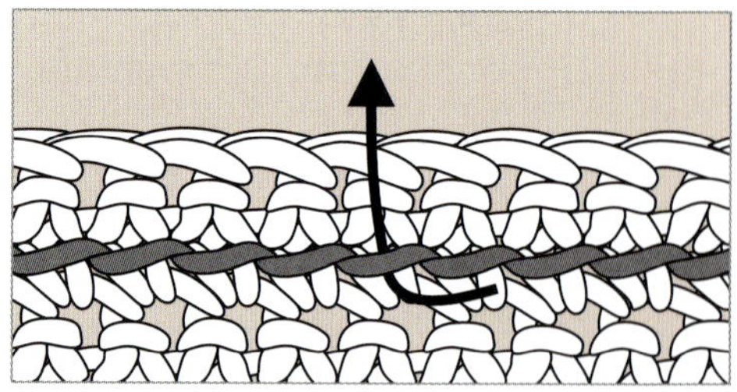

Fig. 2b

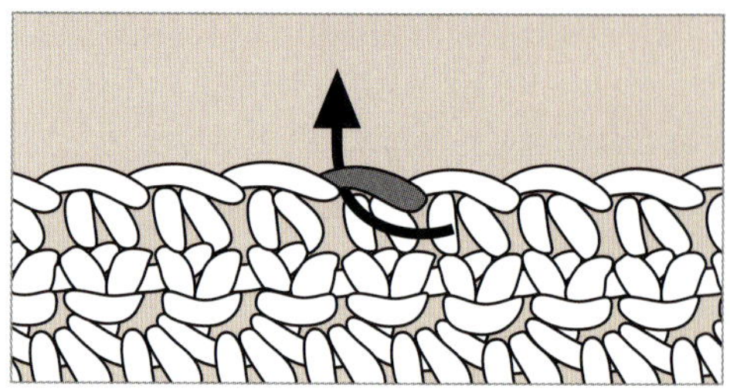

CROCHET TERMINOLOGY		
UNITED STATES		INTERNATIONAL
slip stitch (slip st)	=	single crochet (sc)
single crochet (sc)	=	double crochet (dc)
half double crochet (hdc)	=	half treble crochet (htr)
double crochet (dc)	=	treble crochet (tr)
treble crochet (tr)	=	double treble crochet (dtr)
double treble crochet (dtr)	=	triple treble crochet (ttr)
triple treble crochet (tr tr)	=	quadruple treble crochet (qtr)
skip	=	miss

Yarn Weight Symbol & Names	LACE 0	SUPER FINE 1	FINE 2	LIGHT 3	MEDIUM 4	BULKY 5	SUPER BULKY 6	JUMBO 7
Type of Yarns in Category	Fingering, size 10 crochet thread	Sock, Fingering, Baby	Sport, Baby	DK, Light Worsted	Worsted, Afghan, Aran	Chunky, Craft, Rug	Super Bulky, Roving	Jumbo, Roving
Crochet Gauge* Ranges in Single Crochet to 4" (10 cm)	32-42 sts**	21-32 sts	16-20 sts	12-17 sts	11-14 sts	8-11 sts	6-9 sts	5 sts and fewer
Advised Hook Size Range	Steel*** 6 to 8, Regular hook B-1	B-1 to E-4	E-4 to 7	7 to I-9	I-9 to K-10½	K-10½ to M/N-13	M/N-13 to Q	Q and larger

*GUIDELINES ONLY: The chart above reflects the most commonly used gauges and hook sizes for specific yarn categories.

** Lace weight yarns are usually crocheted with larger hooks to create lacy openwork patterns. Accordingly, a gauge range is difficult to determine. Always follow the gauge stated in your pattern.

*** Steel crochet hooks are sized differently from regular hooks–the higher the number, the smaller the hook, which is the reverse of regular hook sizing.

POST STITCH

Work around post of stitch indicated, inserting hook in direction of arrow *(Fig. 3)*.

Fig. 3

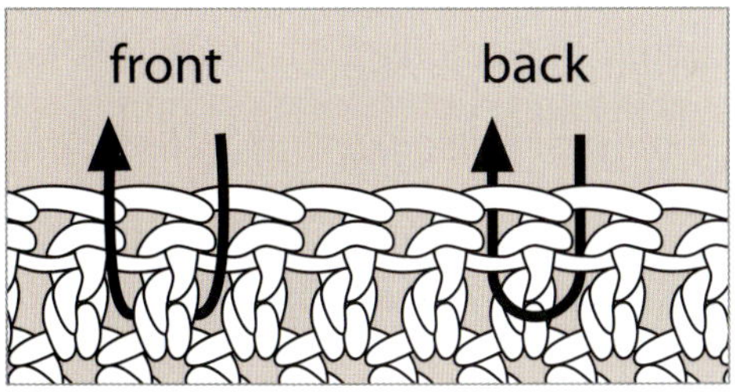

MATTRESS STITCH

With the **right** side of both edges facing you and matching stitches, sew through both sides once to secure the beginning of the seam. Insert the needle from **back** to **front** through **both** loops of stitch on one side ***(Fig. 4a)***, then from **back** to **front** through **both** loops of stitch on other side ***(Fig. 4b)***. Continue in this manner, easing in fullness and drawing seam together as you work to create a flat seam.

Fig. 4a

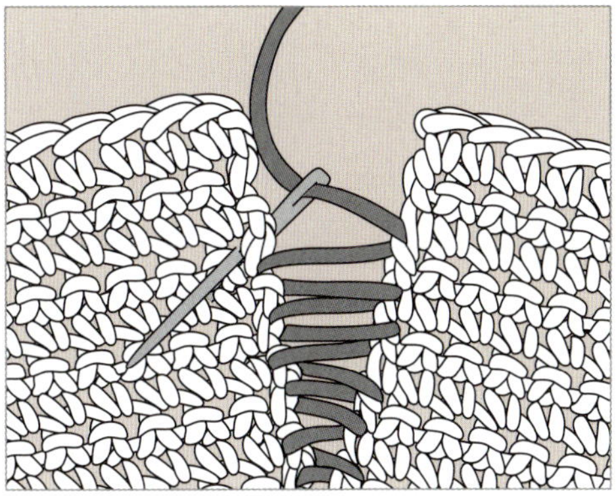

Fig. 4b

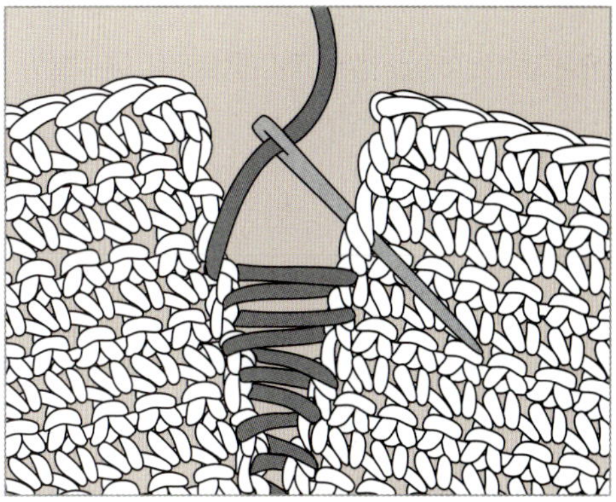

Yarn Information

The Afghans in this book were made using Medium Weight Yarn. Any brand of Medium Weight Yarn may be used. It is best to refer to the yardage/meters when determining how many balls or skeins to purchase. Remember, to arrive at the finished size, it is the GAUGE/TENSION that is important, not the brand of yarn.

For your convenience, listed below are the yarn styles and colors used to create our photography models. Because yarn manufacturers make frequent changes in their product lines, you may sometimes find it necessary to use a substitute yarn or to search for the discontinued product at alternate suppliers (locally or online).

BEAR AFGHAN
Lion Brand® Heartland®
MC - #125 Mammoth Cave
Caron® Simply Soft®
CC - #9701 White **or** #9702 Off White

WOLF AFGHAN
Lion Brand® Heartland®
MC - #135 Yosemite
Caron® Simply Soft®
CC - #9701 White

MOOSE AFGHAN
Lion Brand® Heartland®
MC - #153 Black Canyon
Caron® Simply Soft®
CC - #9701 White

DEER AFGHAN
Lion Brand® Heartland®
MC - #122 Grand Canyon
Caron® Simply Soft®
CC - #9701 White

Meet Christine Naugle

Christine Naugle enjoyed crochet as a hobby from childhood to adulthood but says she really started to love it when her sisters and friends began having babies.

"It was important for me to give them a handmade keepsake for such a special occasion," she said. "I began designing my own patterns in 2011 and haven't looked back."

After growing up on a potato farm in eastern Idaho, Christine earned a degree in Social Science and Public Affairs and became a manager in the corporate world. Now a stay-at-home mom, she manages to create crochet designs (and does custom designing) through her web site, SweetPotato3.com.

Family time with her husband and three children is usually spent doing "all things outdoors," including downhill skiing, camping, hiking, kayaking, biking, and more. "I spend most evenings cheering on my sons who play baseball and my daughter who loves dance," she says. "When I have time to myself, I enjoy running and digital scrapbooking."

Production Team: Instructional/Technical Editor - Linda A. Daley; Editorial Writer - Susan Frantz Wiles; Senior Graphic Artist - Lora Puls; Photo Stylist - Stephanie Moore; and Photographer - Jason Masters.

Made In U.S.A.